ALAN W. WATTS

Beat Zen Square Zen and ZEN

CITY LIGHTS BOOKS

Library of Congress Catalog Card Number: 59-9266

CITY LIGHTS BOOKS are published at 1562 Grant Avenue,
San Francisco, Calif 94133

FOREWORD

THE following essay first appeared in the *Chicago Review* for the Summer of 1958, and is now republished with the Editor's kind permission. To the present version, however, certain additions have been made, because this seemed to be a good context in which to discuss the influence of Zen on Western Art, and because the original was published before the appearance of Kerouac's *Dharma Bums*

I had supposed that the original version of this essay had made my own position with respect to "Beat Zen" and "Square Zen" perfectly clear. It was, of course, obvious that I was not using the word "square" as a taunt since I was not speaking from the standpoint of "beat." But as a result of Stephen Mahoney's article "The Prevalence of Zen" which appeared in *The Nation* in October, 1958, the impression has been circulating that I am a spokesman for "Square Zen." By this term I was designating the traditional and official Zen schools of Japan, Rinzai and Soto, to which many Westerners do indeed belong. I do not, nor do I represent them in any capacity. This is not because I disrespect them or have some quarrel with them, but because in matters of this kind I am temperamentally not a joiner. I do not even style myself a Zen Buddhist. For the aspect of Zen in which I am personally interested is nothing that can be organized, taught, transmitted, certified, or wrapped up in any kind of system. It can't even be followed, for everyone has to find it for himself. As Plotinus said, it is "a flight of the alone to the Alone," and as old Zen poem says:

> If you do not get it from yourself,
> Where will you go for it?

Fundamentally, this is in a sense the position of the whole Zen Buddhist tradition. Strictly speaking, there are no Zen masters because Zen has nothing to teach. From the earliest times those who have experienced Zen have always repulsed would-be disciples, not just to test their sincerity, but to give fair warning that the experience of awakening (*satori*) is not to be found by seeking, and is not in any case something that can be acquired or cultivated. But seekers have persistently refused to take this "No!" for an answer, and to this the Zen sages have responded with a kind of *judo*. Realizing the uselessness of just *telling* the seeker that seeking will not find, they have replied with counter questions (*koan*) which have the effect of exciting the effort of seeking until it explodes with its own force, so that the student realizes the folly of seeking for himself — not just verbally but through to the very marrow of his bones. At this point the student "has" Zen. He knows himself to be one with all, for he is no longer separating himself from the universe by seeking something from it.

On the surface, this looks like a master-disciple relationship. But essentially it is what Buddhists call *upaya* or "skillful means," sometimes known as "giving a yellow leaf to a child to stop it crying for gold." In the course of centuries, however, the process of refusal and counter questioning has become increasingly formal. Temples and institutions have arisen where it may be carried on, and these have in turn created problems of ownership, administration, and discipline compelling Zen Buddhism to assume the form of a traditional hierarchy. In the Far-East this has gone on for so long that it is part of the landscape, and some of its disadvantages are offset by the fact that it seems perfectly natural. There is nothing exotic or "special" about it. Even organizations can grow naturally. But it seems to me that the transplantation of this style of Zen to the West would be completely artificial. It would simply become another of the numerous cult-organizations with their spiritual claims, vested interests, and "in-groups" of followers, with the additional disadvantage of the snob-appeal of being a "very esoteric" form of Buddhism. Let Zen soak into the West informally, like the drinking of tea. We can digest it better that way.

ALAN W. WATTS.

Mill Valley, California
March, 1959

BEAT ZEN, SQUARE ZEN, AND ZEN

It is as difficult for Anglo-Saxons as for the Japanese to absorb anything quite so Chinese as Zen. For though the word "Zen" is Japanese and though Japan is now its home, Zen Buddhism is the creation of T'ang dynasty China. I do not say this as a prelude to harping upon the incommunicable subtleties of alien cultures. The point is simply that people who feel a profound need to justify themselves have difficulty in understanding the view-points of those who do not, and the Chinese who created Zen were the same kind of people as Lao-tzu, who, cen-turies before, had said, "Those who justify themselves do not convince." For the urge to make or prove oneself right has always jiggled the Chinese sense of the ludic-rous, since as both Confucians and Taoists—however dif-ferent these philosophies in other ways—they have in-variably appreciated the man who can "come off it." To Confucius it seemed much better to be human-hearted than righteous, and to the great Taoists, Lao-tzu and Chuang-tzu, it was obvious that one could not be right without also being wrong, because the two were as in-separable as back and front. As Chuang-tzu said, "Those who would have good government without its correlative misrule, and right without its correlative wrong, do not understand the principles of the universe."

To Western ears such words may sound cynical, and the Confucian admiration of "reasonableness" and compromise may appear to be a weak-kneed lack of commitment to principle. Actually they reflect a marvelous understanding and respect for what we call the balance of nature, human and otherwise—a universal vision of life as the Tao or way of nature in which the good and the evil, the creative and the destructive, the wise and the foolish are the inseparable polarities of existence. "Tao," said the *Chung-yung*, "is that from which one cannot depart. That from which one can depart is not the Tao." Therefore wisdom did not consist in trying to wrest the good from the evil but in learning to "ride" them as a cork adapts itself to the crests and troughs of the waves. At the roots of Chinese life there is a trust in the good-and-evil of one's own nature which is peculiarly foreign to those brought up with the chronic uneasy conscience of the Hebrew-Christian cultures. Yet it was always obvious to the Chinese that a man who mistrusts himself cannot even trust his mistrust, and must therefore be hopelessly confused.

For rather different reasons, Japanese people tend to be as uneasy in themselves as Westerners, having a sense of social shame quite as acute as our more metaphysical sense of sin. This was especially true of the class most attracted to Zen, the *samurai*. Ruth Benedict, in that very uneven work *Chrysanthemum and Sword*, was, I think, perfectly correct in saying that the attraction of Zen to the *samurai* class was its power to get rid of an extremely awkward self-consciousness induced in the education of

2

the young. Part-and-parcel of this self-consciousness is the Japanese compulsion to compete with oneself—a compulsion which turns every craft and skill into a marathon of self-discipline. Although the attraction of Zen lay in the possibility of liberation from self-consciousness, the Japanese version of Zen fought fire with fire, overcoming the "self observing the self" by bringing it to an intensity in which it exploded. How remote from the regimen of the Japanese Zen monastery are the words of the great T'ang master Lin-chi:

> In Buddhism there is no place for using effort. Just be ordinary and nothing special. Eat your food, move your bowels, pass water, and when you're tired go and lie down. The ignorant will laugh at me, but the wise will understand.

Yet the spirit of these words is just as remote from a kind of Western Zen which would employ this philosophy to justify a very self-defensive Bohemianism.

There is no single reason for the extraordinary growth of Western interest in Zen during the last twenty years. The appeal of Zen arts to the "modern" spirit in the West, the work of Suzuki, the war with Japan, the itchy fascination of "Zen-stories," and the attraction of a nonconceptual, experiential philosophy in the climate of scientific relativism—all these are involved. One might mention, too, the affinities between Zen and such purely Western trends as the philosophy of Wittgenstein, Existentialism, General Semantics, the metalinguistics of B. L. Whorf, and certain movements in the philosophy of science and in psychotherapy. Always in the background there is our vague disquiet with the artificialty or "antinaturalness" of both Christianity, with its politically ordered cosmology, and technology, with its imperialistic mechanization of a natural world from which man himself feels strangely alien. For both reflect a psychology in which man is identified with a conscious intelligence and will standing apart from nature to control it, like the architect-God in whose image this version of man is conceived. The disquiet arises from the suspicion that our attempt to master the world from outside is a vicious circle in which we shall be condemned to the perpetual insomnia of controlling controls and supervising supervision *ad infinitum*.

To the Westerner in search of the reintegration of man and nature there is an appeal far beyond the merely sentimental in the naturalism of Zen—in the landscapes of Ma-yuan and Sesshu, in an art which is simultaneously spiritual and secular, which conveys the mystical in terms of the natural, and which, indeed, never even imagined a break between them. Here is a view of the world imparting a profoundly refreshing sense of wholeness to a culture in which the spiritual and the material, the conscious and the unconscious, have been cataclysmically split. For this reason the Chinese humanism and naturalism of Zen intrigue us much more strongly than Indian Buddhism or Vedanta. These, too, have their students in the West, but their followers seem for the most part to be displaced Christians — people in search of a more plausible philosophy than Christian supernaturalism to carry on the essentially Christian search for the miraculous. The ideal man of Indian Buddhism is clearly a superman, a *yogi* with absolute mastery of his own nature, according perfectly with the science-fiction ideal of "men beyond mankind." But the Buddha or awakened man of Chinese Zen is "ordinary and nothing special"; he is humorously human like the Zen tramps portrayed by Mu-chi and Liang-k'ai. We like this because here, for the first time, is a conception of the holy man and sage who is not impossibly remote, not superhuman but fully human, and, above all, not a solemn and sexless ascetic. Furthermore, in Zen the *satori* experience of awakening to our "original inseparability" with the universe seems, however elusive, always just round the corner. One has even met people to whom it has happened, and they are no longer mysterious occultists in the Himalayas nor skinny *yogis* in cloistered *ashrams*. They are just like us, and yet much more at home in the world, floating much more easily upon the ocean of transience and insecurity.

Above all, I believe that Zen appeals to many in the post-Christian West because it does not preach, moralize, and scold in the style of Hebrew-Christian prophetism. Buddhism does not deny that there is a relatively limited sphere in which human life may be improved by art and science, reason and good-will. However, it regards this sphere of activity as important but nonetheless subordinate to the comparatively limitless sphere in which things are as they are, always have been, and always will be— a sphere entirely beyond the categories of good and evil, success and failure, and individual health and sickness. On the one hand, this is the sphere of the great universe. Looking out into it at night, we make no comparisons between right and wrong stars, nor between well and badly arranged constellations. Stars are by nature big and little, bright and dim. Yet the whole thing is a splendor and a marvel which sometimes makes our flesh creep

5

with awe. On the other hand, this is also the sphere of human, everyday life which we might call existential.

For there is a standpoint from which human affairs are as much beyond right and wrong as the stars, and from which our deeds, experiences, and feelings can no more be judged than the ups and downs of a range of mountains. Though beyond moral and social valuation, this level of human life may also be seen to be just as marvelous and uncanny as the great universe itself. This feeling may become particularly acute when the individual ego tries to fathom its own nature, to plumb the inner sources of its own actions and consciousness. For here it discovers a part of itself—the inmost and greatest part— which is strange to itself and beyond its understanding and control. Odd as it may sound, the ego finds that its own center and nature is beyond itself. The more deeply I go into myself, the more I am not myself, and yet this is the very heart of me. Here I find my own inner workings functioning of themselves, spontaneously, like the rotation of the heavenly bodies and the drifting of the clouds. Strange and foreign as this aspect of myself at first seems to be, I soon realize that it *is* me, and much more me than my superficial ego. This is not fatalism or determinism, because there is no longer anyone being pushed around or determined; there is nothing that this deep "I" is not doing. The configuration of my nervous-system, like the configuration of the stars, happens of itself, and this "itself" is the real "myself."

From this standpoint—and here language reveals its limitations with a vengeance—I find that I cannot help doing and experiencing, quite freely, what is always "right," in the sense that the stars are always in their "right" places. As Hsiang-yen put it,

> There's no use for artificial discipline,
> For, move as I will, I manifest the ancient Tao.

At this level, human life is beyond anxiety, for it can never make a mistake. If we live, we live; if we die, we die; if we suffer, we suffer; if we are terrified, we are terrified. There is no problem about it. A Zen "master" was once asked, "It is terribly hot, and how shall we escape the heat?" "Why not," he answered, "go to the place where it is neither hot or cold?" "Where is that place?" "In summer we sweat; in winter we shiver." In Zen one does not feel guilty about dying, or being afraid, or disliking the heat. At the same time, Zen does not insist upon this point of view as something which one *ought* to adopt; it does not preach it as an ideal. For if you don't understand it, your very not understanding is also IT. There would be no bright stars without dim stars, and, without the surrounding darkness, no stars at all.

The Hebrew-Christian universe is one in which moral urgency, the anxiety to be right, embraces and penetrates everything. God, the Absolute itself, is good as against bad, and thus to be immoral or in the wrong is to feel oneself an outcast not merely from human society but also from existence itself, from the root and ground of life. To be in the wrong therefore arouses a metaphysical anxiety and sense of guilt—a state of eternal damnation— utterly disproportionate to the crime. This metaphysical guilt is so insupportable that it must eventually issue in the rejection of God and of his laws—which is just what has happened in the whole movement of modern secularism, materialism, and naturalism. Absolute morality is profoundly destructive of morality, for the sanctions which it invokes against evil are far, far too heavy. One does not cure the headache by cutting off the head. The appeal of Zen, as of other forms of Eastern philosophy, is that it unveils behind the urgent realm of good and evil a vast region of oneself about which there need be no guilt or recrimination, where at last the self is indistinguishable from God.

But the Westerner who is attracted by Zen and who would understand it deeply must have one indispensable qualification: he must understand his own culture so thoroughly that he is no longer swayed by its premises unconsciously. He must really have come to terms with the Lord God Jehovah and with his Hebrew-Christian conscience so that he can take it or leave it without fear or rebellion. He must be free of the itch to justify himself. Lacking this, his Zen will be either "beat" or "square," either a revolt from the culture and social order or a new form of stuffiness and respectability. For Zen is above all the liberation of the mind from conventional thought, and this is something utterly different from rebellion against convention, on the one hand, or adapting foreign conventions, on the other.

Conventional thought is, in brief, the confusion of the concrete universe of nature with the conceptual things, events, and values of linguistic and cultural symbolism. For in Taoism and Zen the world is seen as an inseparably interrelated field or continuum, no part of which can actually be separated from the rest or valued above or below the rest. It was in this sense that Hui-neng, the Sixth Patriarch, meant that "fundamentally not one thing exists," for he realized that things are *terms* not entities. They exist in the abstract world of thought, but not in the concrete world of nature. Thus one who actually perceives or feels this to be so no longer feels that he is an ego, except by definition. He sees that his ego is his *persona* or social role, a somewhat arbitrary selection of experiences with which he has been taught to identify himself. (Why, for example, do we say "I think" but not "I am beating my heart"?) Having seen this, he continues to play his social role without being taken in by it. He does not precipitately adopt a new role or play the role of having no role at all. He plays it cool.

The "beat" mentality as I am thinking of it is something much more extensive and vague than the hipster life of New York and San Francisco. It is a younger generation's nonparticipation in "the American Way of Life," a revolt which does not seek to change the existing order but simply turns away from it to find the significance of life in subjective experience rather than objective achievement. It contrasts with the "square" and other-directed mentality of beguilement by social convention, unaware of the correlativity of right and wrong, of the mutual necessity of capitalism and communism to each other's existence, of the inner identity of puritanism and lechery, or of, say, the alliance of church lobbies and organized crime to maintain laws against gambling.

Beat Zen is a complex phenomenon. It ranges from a use of Zen for justifying sheer caprice in art, literature, and life to a very forceful social criticism and "digging of the universe" such as one may find in the poetry of Ginsberg, Whalen and Snyder, and, rather unevenly, in Kerouac, who is always a shade too self-conscious, too subjective, and too strident to have the flavor of Zen.

When Kerouac gives his philosophical final statement, "I don't know. I don't care. And it doesn't make any difference"— the cat is out of the bag, for there is a hostility in these words which clangs with self-defense. But just because Zen truly surpasses convention and its values, it has no need to say "To hell with it," nor to underline with violence the fact that anything goes.

It is indeed the basic intuition of Zen that there is an ultimate standpoint from which "anything goes." In the celebrated words of the master Yun-men, "Every day is a good day." Or as is said in the *Hsin-hsin Ming:*

> If you want to get the plain truth,
> Be not concerned with right and wrong.
> The conflict between right and wrong
> Is the sickness of the mind.

But this standpoint does not exclude and is not hostile towards the distinction between right and wrong at other levels and in more limited frames of reference. The world is seen to be beyond right and wrong when it is not framed: that is to say, when we are not looking at a particular situation by itself—out of relation to the rest of the universe. Within this room there is a clear difference between up and down; out in interstellar space there is not. Within the conventional limits of a human community there are clear distinctions between good and evil. But these disappear when human affairs are seen as part and parcel of the whole realm of nature. Every framework sets up a restricted field of relationships, and restriction is law or rule.

Now a skilled photographer can point his camera at almost any scene or object and create a marvelous composition by the way in which he frames and lights it. An unskilled photographer attempting the same thing creates only messes, for he does not know how to place the frame, the border of the picture, where it will be in relation to the contents. How eloquently this demonstrates that as soon as we introduce a frame anything does *not* go. But every work of art involves a frame. A frame of some kind is precisely what distinguishes a painting, a poem, a musical composition, a play, a dance, or a piece of sculpture from the rest of the world. Some artists may argue that they do not want their works to be distinguishable from the total universe, but if this be so they should not frame them in galleries and concert halls. Above all they should not sign them nor sell them. This is as immoral as selling the moon or signing one's name to a mountain. (Such an artist may perhaps be forgiven if he knows what he is doing, and prides himself inwardly, not on being a poet or painter, but a competent crook.) Only destructive little boys and vulgar excursionists go around initialling the trees.

Today there are Western artists avowedly using Zen to justify the indiscriminate framing of simply anything—blank canvases, totally silent music, torn up bits of paper dropped on a board and stuck where they fall, or dense masses of mangled wire. The work of the composer John Cage is rather typical of this tendency. In the name of Zen, he has forsaken his earlier and promising work with the "prepared piano," to confront audiences with eight Ampex tape-recorders simultaneously bellowing forth random noises. There is, indeed, a considerable therapeutic value in allowing oneself to be deeply aware of any sight or sound that may arise. For one thing, it brings to mind the marvel of seeing and hearing as such. For another, the profound willingness to listen to or gaze upon anything at all frees the mind from fixed preconceptions of beauty, creating, as it were, a free space in which altogether new forms and relationships may emerge. But this is therapy; it is not yet art. It is on the level of the random ramblings of a patient on the analyst's couch: very important indeed as therapy, though it is by no means the aim of psychoanalysis to substitute such ramblings for conversation and literature. Cage's work would be redeemed if he framed and presented it as a kind of group session in audio-therapy, but as a concert it is simply absurd. One may hope, however, that *after* Cage has, by such listening, set his own mind free from the composer's almost inevitable plagiarism of the forms of the past, he will present us with the new musical patterns and relationships which he has not yet uttered.

Just as the skilled photographer often amazes us with his lighting and framing of the most unlikely subjects, so there are painters and writers in the West, as well as in modern Japan, who have mastered the authentically Zen art of controlling accidents. Historically this first arose in the Far-East in the appreciation of the rough texture of brush-strokes in calligraphy and painting, and in the accidental running of the glaze on bowls made for the tea-ceremony. One of the classical instances of this kind of thing came about through the shattering of a fine ceramic tea-caddy, belonging to one of the old Japanese tea-masters. The fragments were cemented together with gold, and its owner was amazed at the way in which the random network of thin gold lines enhanced its beauty. It must be remembered, however, that this was an *objet trouvé*—an accidental effect *selected* by a man of exquisite taste, and treasured as one might treasure and exhibit a marvelous rock or a piece of driftwood. For in the Zen-inspired art of *bonseki* or rock-gardening, the stones are selected with infinite care, and though the hand of man may never have changed them it is far from true that any old stone will do. Furthermore, in calligraphy, painting, and ceramics, the accidental effects of running glaze or of flying hair-lines of the brush were only accepted and presented by the artist when he felt them to be fortuitous and unexpected marvels within the context of the work as a whole.

What governed his judgement? What gives *certain* accidental effects in painting the same beauty as the accidental outlines of clouds? According to Zen feeling there is no precise rule, no rule, that is to say, which can be formulated in words and taught systematically. On the other hand, there is in all these things a principle of order which in Chinese philosophy is termed *li,* and which Joseph Needham has translated "organic pattern." *Li* originally meant the markings in jade, the grain in wood, and the fiber in muscle. It designates a type of order which is too multi-dimensional, too subtly interrelated, and too squirmingly vital to be represented in words or mechanical images. The artist has to know it as he knows how to grow his hair. He can do it again and again, but can never explain how. In Taoist philosophy this power is called *te,* or "magical virtue." It is the element of the miraculous which we feel both at the stars in heaven and at our own ability to be conscious.

It is the possession of *te,* then, which makes all the difference between mere scrawls and the "white writing" of Mark Tobey which admittedly derived its inspiration from Chinese calligraphy. It was by no means a purely haphazard drooling of paint or uncontrolled wandering of the brush, for the character and taste of such an artist is visible in the grace (a possible equivalent of *te*) with which his strokes are formed even when he is not trying to represent anything except strokes. It is also what makes the difference between mere patches, smudges, and trails of black ink and the work of such Japanese moderns as Sabro Hasegawa and Onchi, which is after all in the *haboku* or "rough style" tradition of Sesshu. Anyone can write absolutely illegible Japanese, but who so enchantingly as Ryokwan? If it is true that "when the wrong man uses the right means, the right means work in the wrong way," it is often also true that when the right man uses the wrong means, the wrong means work in the right way.

The real genius of Chinese and Japanese Zen artists in their use of controlled accidents goes beyond the discovery of fortuitous beauty. It lies in being able to express, at the level of artistry, the realization of that ultimate standpoint from which "anything goes" and at which "all things are of one suchness." The mere selection of any random shape to stick in a frame simply confuses the metaphysical and the artistic domains; it does not express the one in terms of the other. Set in a frame, any old mess is at once cut off from the totality of its natural context, and for this very reason its manifestation of the Tao is concealed. The formless murmer of night noises in a great city has an enchantment which immediately disappears when formally presented as music in a concert hall. A frame outlines a universe, a microcosm, and if the contents of the frame are to rank as art they must have the same quality of relationship to the whole and to each other as events in the great universe, the macrocosm of nature. In nature the accidental is always recognized in relation to what is ordered and controlled. The dark *yin* is never without the bright *yang*. Thus the painting of Sesshu, the calligraphy of Ryokwan, and the ceramic bowls of the Hagi or Karatsu schools reveal the wonder of accidents in nature through accidents in a context of highly disciplined art.

The realization of the unswerving "rightness" of whatever happens is no more manifested by utter lawlessness in social conduct than by sheer caprice in art. As Zen has been used as a pretext for the latter in our times, its use as a pretext for the former is ancient history. Many a rogue has justified himself with the Buddhist formula, "Birth-and-death *(samsara)* is Nirvana; worldly passions are Enlightenment." This danger is implicit in Zen because it is implicit in freedom. Power and freedom can never be safe. They are dangerous in the same way that fire and electricity are dangerous. But it is quite pitiful to see Zen used as a pretext for license when the Zen in question is no more than an idea in the head, a simple rationalization. To some extent "Zen" is so used in the underworld which often attaches itself to artistic and intellectual communities. After all, the Bohemian way of life is primarily the natural consequence of artists and writers being so absorbed in their work that they have no interest in keeping up with the Joneses. It is also a symptom of creative changes in manners and morals which at first seem as reprehensible to conservatives as new forms in art. But every such community attracts a number of weak imitators and hangers-on, especially in the great cities, and it is mostly in this class that one now finds the stereotype of the "beatnik" with his phony Zen. Yet if Zen were not the pretext for this shiftless existence, it would be something else.

Is it, then, this underworld which is described in Kerouac's *Dharma Bums?* It is generally known that *The Dharma Bums* is not a novel but a flimsily fictionized account of the author's experiences in California in 1956. To anyone who knows the milieu described, the identity of each character is plain and it is no secret that Japhy Ryder, the hero of the story, is Gary Snyder.* Whatever may be said of Kerouac himself and of a few other characters in the story, it would be difficult indeed to fit Snyder into any stereotype of the Bohemian underworld. He has spent a year of Zen study in Kyoto, and has recently (1959) returned for another session, perhaps for two years this time. He is also a serious student of Chinese, having studied with Shih-hsiang Chen at the University of California, and superbly translated a number of the poems of the Zen hermit Han Shan.* His own work scattered through many periodicals, entitles him to be re-

---

The names were changed at the last minute, and at one point "Gary" remains instead of "Japhy." The excerpt published in the Summer 1958 CHICAGO REVIEW under the title "Meditation in the Woods" keeps the original names.

"Cold Mountain Poems," EVERGREEN REVIEW, vol. 2, no 6, 1958.

garded as one of the finest poets of the San Francisco renaissance.

But Snyder is, in the best sense, a bum. His manner of life is a quietly individualistic deviation from everything expected of a "good consumer." His temporary home is a little shack without utilities on a hillside in Mill Valley, at the top of a steep trail. When he needs money he goes to sea, or works as a firewatcher or logger. Otherwise, he stays at home or goes mountain-climbing, most of the time writing, studying, or practicing Zen meditation. Part of his shack is set aside as a formal "meditation hall," and the whole place is in the best Zen tradition of clean and uncluttered simplicity. But this is not a Christian or Hinayana Buddhist style of asceticism. As *The Dharma Bums* made plain, it combines a voluntary and rather joyous poverty with a rich love-life, and for Western, and much Eastern, religiosity this is the touchstone of deviltry. This is not the place to argue the complex problem of spirituality and sexuality,* but one can only say, "So much the worse for such religiosity." This attitude has seldom been a part of Zen, new or old, beat or square.

In *The Dharma Bums,* however, we are seeing Snyder through Kerouac's eyes, and some distortions arise because Kerouac's own Buddhism is a true beat Zen which confuses "anything goes" at the existential level with "anything goes" on the artistic and social levels. Nevertheless, there is something endearing about Kerouac's personality as a writer, something which comes out in the warmth of his admiration for Gary, and in the lusty,

*For which see Part II of my NATURE, MAN, AND WOMAN. New York. 1958.

generous enthusiasm for life which wells up at every point in his colorful and wholly undisciplined prose. This exuberent warmth makes it impossible to put Kerouac in the class of the beat mentality described by John Clelland-Holmes—the cool, fake-intellectual hipster searching for kicks, name-dropping bits of Zen and jazz jargon to justify a disaffiliation from society which is in fact just ordinary, callous exploitation of other people. In the North Beach, Greenwich Village, and elsewhere such characters may occasionally be found, but no one has ever heard of any of them, and their identification with the active artists and poets of these communities is pure journalistic imagination. They are, however, the shadow of a substance, the low-level caricature which always attends spiritual and cultural movements, carrying them to extremes which their authors never intended. To this extent beat Zen is sowing confusion in idealizing as art and life what should be kept to oneself as therapy.

One of the most problematic characteristics of beat Zen, shared to some extent both by the creative artists and their imitators, is the fascination for marijuana and peyote, and the notion that the states of consciousness produced by these substances have some affinity with *satori*. That many of these people "take drugs" naturally lays them wide open to the most extreme forms of righteous indignation, despite the fact that marijuana and peyote (or its derivative, mescaline) are far less harmful and habit-forming than whiskey or tobacco. But while it is true that these drugs induce states of great aesthetic insight and, perhaps, therapeutic value, the *satori*-experience is so startlingly different from anything of this kind that no one who had shared both could possibly confuse

18

them. Both states of consciousness require an apparently paradoxical type of language to describe them, for which reason one might easily confuse the drug-induced states with written accounts of *satori*. But *satori* is always marked by a kind of intense clarity and simplicity from which complex imagery, jazzed-up sense perceptions, and the strange "turned-on" feeling invariably produced by these drugs are absent. It is not by chance that *satori* is called *fu-sho* or "unproduced," which means, among other things, that there is no gimmick whether psychological or chemical for bringing it about. *Satori* always remains inaccessible to the mind preoccupied with its own states or with the search for ecstasy.

Now the underlying protestant lawlessness of beat Zen disturbs the square Zennists very seriously. For square Zen is the Zen of established tradition in Japan with its clearly defined hierarchy, its rigid discipline, and its specific tests of *satori*. More particularly, it is the kind of Zen adopted by Westerners studying in Japan, who will before long be bringing it back home. But there is an obvious difference between square Zen and the common-or-garden squareness of the Rotary Club or the Presbyterian Church. It is infinitely more imaginative, sensitive and interesting. But it is still square because it is a quest for the *right* spiritual experience, for a *satori* which will receive the stamp *(inka)* of approval and established authority. There will even be certificates to hang on the wall.

If square Zen falls into any serious excess it is in the direction of spiritual snobbism and artistic preciousness, though I have never known an orthodox Zen teacher who could be accused of either. These gentlemen seem to take

19

their exalted office rather lightly, respecting its dignity without standing on it. The faults of square Zen are the faults of any spiritual in-group with an esoteric discipline and degrees of initiation. Students in the lower ranks can get unpleasantly uppity about inside knowledge which they are not at liberty to divulge—"and you wouldn't understand even if I could tell you"—and are apt to dwell rather sickeningly on the immense difficulties and iron disciplines of their task. There are times, however, when this is understandable, especially when someone who is just goofing-off claims that he is following the Zen ideal of "naturalness."

The student of square Zen is also inclined at times to be niggling in his recognition of parallels to Zen in other spiritual traditions. Because the essentials of Zen can never be accurately and fully formulated, being an experience and not a set of ideas, it is always possible to be critical of anything anyone says about it, neither putting up nor shutting up. Any statement about Zen, or about spiritual experience of any kind, will always leave some aspect, some subtlety, unexpressed. Noone's mouth is big enough to utter the whole thing. The Western follower of Zen should also resist the temptation to associate himself with an even worse form of snobbery, the intellectual snobbery so largely characteristic of Far-Eastern studies in American universities. In this particular field the fad for making humanistic studies "scientific" has gone to such wild extremes that even Suzuki is accused of being a "popularizer" instead of a serious scholar—presumably because he is a little unsystematic about footnotes and covers a vast area instead of confining himself with rigor to a single problem. *e.g.,* "An

Analysis of Some Illegible and Archaic Character-forms in the Tun-huang Manuscript of the Sutra of the Sixth Patriarch." There is a proper and honorable place in scholarship for the meticulous drudge, but when he is on top instead of on tap his dangerous envy of real intelligence drives all creative scholars from the field.*

In its artistic expression square Zen is often rather tediously studied and precious, a fate which all too easily befalls a venerable aesthetic tradition when its techniques are so highly developed that it takes a lifetime to master any one of them. No one has then the time to go beyond the achievements of the old masters, so that new generations are condemned to endless repetition and imitation of their refinements. The student of *sumi*-painting, calligraphy, *haiku*-poetry, or tea-ceremony can therefore get trapped in a tiresomely repetitious affectation of styles, varied only with increasingly esoteric allusions to the work of the past. When this comes to the point of imitating the old masters' happy accidents in such a way that "primitive" and "rough" effects are produced by the utmost practice and deliberation, the whole thing becomes so painful that even the wildest excesses of beat Zen art look refreshing. Indeed, it is possible that beat Zen and square Zen will so complement and rub against

---

Suzuki, incidentally, is a very rare bird among contemporary Asians—an original thinker. He is no mere mouthpiece for any fixed tradition, and has come forth with some ideas about comparative religion and the psychology of religion which are of enormous importance, quite aside from what he has done to translate and interpret the literature of Zen. But it is just for this reason that people in square Zen and academic sinology have their qualms about accepting him.

one another that an amazingly pure and lively Zen will arise from the hassle.

For this reason I see no really serious quarrel with either extreme. There was never a spiritual movement without its excesses and distortions. The experience of awakening which truly constitutes Zen is too timeless and universal to be injured. The extremes of beat Zen need alarm no one since, as Blake said, "the fool who persists in his folly will become wise." As for square Zen, "authoritative" spiritual experiences have always had a way of wearing thin, and thus of generating the demand for something genuine and unique which needs no stamp.

I have known followers of both extremes to come up with perfectly clear *satori* experiences, for since there is no real "way" to *satori* the way you are following makes very little difference.

But the quarrel *between* the extremes is of great philosophical interest, being a contemporary form of the ancient dispute between salvation by works and salvation by faith, or between what the Hindus called the ways of the monkey and the cat. The cat—appropriately enough—follows the effortless way, since the mother cat carries her kittens. The monkey follows the hard way, since the baby monkey has to hang on to its mother's hair. Thus for beat Zen there must be no effort, no discipline, no artificial striving to attain *satori* or to be anything but what one is. But for square Zen there can be no true *satori* without years of meditation-practice under the stern supervision of a qualified master. In seventeenth-century Japan these two attitudes were *approximately* typified by the great masters Bankei and Hakuin, and it so happens that the followers of the latter "won out" and determined the present-day character of Rinzai Zen.*

Satori can lie along both roads. It is the concomitant of a "non-grasping" attitude of the senses to experience, and grasping can be exhausted by the discipline of directing its utmost intensity to a single, ever-elusive objective. But what makes the way of effort and will-power suspect to many Westerners is not so much an inherent laziness as a thorough familiarity with the wisdom of our own culture. The square Western Zennists are often quite naive when it comes to an understanding of Christian theology or of all that has been discovered in modern psychiatry, for both have long been concerned with the fallibility and unconscious ambivalence of the will. Both have posed problems as to the vicious circle of seeking self-surrender or of "free-associating on purpose" or of accepting one's conflicts to escape from them, and to anyone who knows anything about either Christianity or psychotherapy these are very real problems. The interest of Chinese Zen and of people like Bankei is that they deal with these problems in a most direct and stimulating way, and begin to suggest some answers. But when Herrigel's Japanese archery master was asked, "How can I give up purpose on purpose?" he replied that no one had ever asked him that before. He had no answer ex-

*Rinzai Zen is the form most widely known in the West. There is also Soto Zen which differs somewhat in technique, but is still closer to Hakuin than to Bankei. However, Bankei should not exactly be identified with beat Zen as I have described it, for he was certainly no advocate of the life of undisciplined whimsy despite all that he said about the importance of the uncalculated life and the folly of seeking Satori.

cept to go on trying blindly, for five years.

Foreign religions can be immensely attractive and highly overrated by those who know little of their own, and especially by those who have not worked through and grown out of their own. This is why the displaced or unconscious Christian can so easily use either beat or square Zen to justify himself. The one wants a philosophy to justify him in doing what he pleases. The other wants a more plausible authoritative salvation than the Church or the psychiatrists seem to be able to provide. Furthermore the atmosphere of Japanese Zen is free from all one's unpleasant childhood associations with God the Father and Jesus Christ—though I know many young Japanese who feel just the same way about their early training in Buddhism. But the true character of Zen remains almost incomprehensible to those who have not surpassed the immaturity of needing to be justified, whether before the Lord God or before a paternalistic society.

The old Chinese Zen masters were steeped in Taoism. They saw nature in its total interrelatedness, and saw that every creature and every experience is in accord with the Tao of nature just as it is. This enabled them to accept themselves as they were, moment by moment, without the least need to justify anything. They didn't do it to defend themselves or to find an excuse for getting away with murder. They didn't brag about it and set themselves apart as rather special. On the contrary, their Zen was *wu-shih*, which means approximately "nothing special" or "no fuss." But Zen is "fuss" when it is mixed up with Bohemian affectations, and "fuss" when it is imagined that the only proper way to find it is to run off to a mon-

24

astery in Japan or to do special exercises in the lotus posture for five hours a day. And I will admit that the very hullabaloo about Zen, even in such an essay as this, is also fuss—but a little less so.

Having said that, I would like to say something for all Zen fussers, beat or square. Fuss is all right, too. If you are hung on Zen, there's no need to try to pretend that you are not. If you really want to spend some years in a Japanese monastery, there is no earthly reason why you shouldn't. Or if you want to spend your time hopping freight cars and digging Charlie Parker, it's a free country.

> In the landscape of Spring there is neither better
>   nor worse;
> The flowering branches grow naturally, some long,
>   some short.